AF270685

African Painted Dogs

Julie Murray

Abdo Kids Junior
is an Imprint of Abdo Kids
abdobooks.com

Abdo
INTERESTING ANIMALS
Kids

abdobooks.com

Published by Abdo Kids, a division of ABDO, P.O. Box 398166, Minneapolis, Minnesota 55439.
Copyright © 2023 by Abdo Consulting Group, Inc. International copyrights reserved in all countries.
No part of this book may be reproduced in any form without written permission from the publisher.
Abdo Kids Junior™ is a trademark and logo of Abdo Kids.

Printed in the United States of America, North Mankato, Minnesota.

102022

012023

Photo Credits: Getty Images, Shutterstock

Production Contributors: Teddy Borth, Jennie Forsberg, Grace Hansen

Design Contributors: Candice Keimig, Pakou Moua

Library of Congress Control Number: 2022937164
Publisher's Cataloging-in-Publication Data

Names: Murray, Julie, author.
Title: African painted dogs / by Julie Murray
Description: Minneapolis, Minnesota : Abdo Kids, 2023 | Series: Interesting animals | Includes online
    resources and index.
Identifiers: ISBN 9781098264123 (lib. bdg.) | ISBN 9781098264680 (ebook) | ISBN 9781098264963
    (Read-to-Me ebook)
Subjects: LCSH: African wild dog--Juvenile literature. | Dogs--Juvenile literature. | Dogs--Behavior--
    Juvenile literature. | Animals--Juvenile literature. | Zoology--Juvenile literature.
Classification: DDC 599.77--dc23

Table of Contents

African Painted Dogs

African painted dogs live
in Africa.

North America
Europe
Asia
Africa
South America
Australia
N
S
E
W

5

They can be found in Africa's

open **plains**.

They are tall and lean. They can weigh 70 pounds (32 kg).

Their fur is black, tan,

and white.

They have big ears.

Their teeth are sharp!

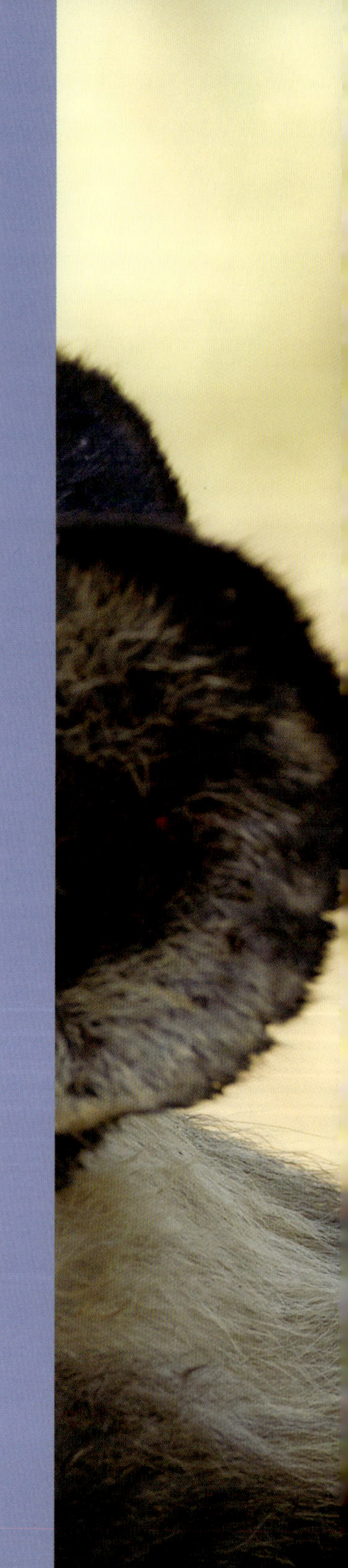

13

They are fast! They can run

45 miles per hour (72 kph).

They live in groups called packs.

17

They hunt in packs.

They chase their **prey**.

18

They eat antelope. They also eat wildebeests and birds.

African Painted Dog Features

big ears

multi-colored fur

sharp teeth

tall and lean

Glossary

plain
a large, flat area of land with few or no trees, sometimes covered by long grass.

prey
an animal hunted by another animal for food.

Index

Abdo Kids
ONLINE
FREE! ONLINE MULTIMEDIA RESOURCES

Visit **abdokids.com** to access crafts, games, videos, and more!

Use Abdo Kids code

IAK4123

or scan this QR code!